P9-BBT-864

DISCARDED

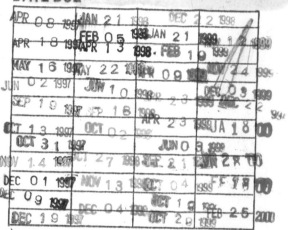

DATE DUE

APR 08 1997	JAN 21 1998	DEC 22 1998	
APR 18 1997	FEB 05 1998 JAN 21 1999		JAN 12 1999
	APR 13 1998 FEB 19 1999		
MAY 16 1997	MAY 22 1998 NOV 09 1998	NOV 24 1999	
JUN 02 1997	JUN 10 1998 APR 23 1999	DEC 09 1999	
SEP 19 1997	SEP 18 1998		DEC 22 1999
OCT 13 1997	OCT 02 1998 APR 23 1999	JA 18 00	
OCT 31 1997		JUN 03 1999	
NOV 14 1997	OCT 27 1998 SEP 21 1999	JAN 28 00	
DEC 01 1997	NOV 13 1998 OCT 04 1999	FE 18 00	
DEC 09 1997	DEC 04 1998 OCT 18 1999	FEB 25 2000	
DEC 19 1997	OCT 28 1999		

MAR 24 2000

APR 05 200

DEMCO

Beginning

SNOWBOARDING

Jon Lurie, Jimmy Clarke, and the following athletes were photographed for this book:
Janine Avent,
Amy Campion,
Dan Dhruva,
Dylan Farr,
Clark Hurlbut,
Bruce Mullinax,
Leslee Olson,
Trevor Phillips,
Sabrina Sadeghi,
Casey Savage,
Forrest Wieland.

Beginning
SNOWBOARDING

Julie Jensen

Adapted from Jon Lurie's
Fundamental Snowboarding

Photographs by Jimmy Clarke

Lerner Publications Company ● Minneapolis

Library of Congress Cataloging-in-Publication Data

Jensen, Julie, 1957–
    Beginning snowboarding / Julie Jensen ; adapted from Jon Lurie's Fundamental snowboarding ; photographs by Jimmy Clarke.
        p. cm. — (Beginning sports)
    Includes bibliographical references (p.   ) and index.
    Summary: Gives an overview of the history, equipment, techniques, competitions, and difficulties associated with the relatively new sport of snowboarding.
    ISBN 0-8225-3507-6 (alk. paper)
    1. Snowboarding — Juvenile literature. [1. Snowboarding.] I. Clarke, Jimmy, ill. II. Lurie, Jon. Fundamental snowboarding.
III. Title. IV. Series.
GV857.S57J45 1996
796.9 — dc20   95-23136

Manufactured in the United States of America

1 2 3 4 5 6 HP 01 00 99 98 97 96

Photo Acknowledgments

Photographs reproduced with the permission of: pp. 8, 38, 59, ALLSPORT/Mike Powell; pp. 9, 10, 15 (all), 18, 19, 21, 58, 63, Burton Snowboards; p. 11, Courtesy of Tom Sims; pp. 40, 61, Courtesy of Chris Thorson; pp. 51, 53 (top right), Photo by Mark Gallup.

Diagram by Laura Westlund.

Contents

Chapter 1

HOW THIS SPORT GOT STARTED

Snowboarders slide smoothly down mountain slopes. They spray snow high into the air. They fly into the air and land on soft, white snow. They twist and turn on hard-packed snow. Snowboarders borrow tricks and skills from surfers, skiers, and skateboarders to create their own special sport.

People have been trying to surf on snow ever since the 1920s. Snowboarding really got started, however, in 1965 when Sherman Poppen invented the Snurfer. He bolted two skis together. The person riding the

Color-Coded Snow

Ski slopes are labeled easy, intermediate, or difficult for skiers and snowboarders. A slope's label depends on how steep it is, whether it has bumps (called moguls), and how wide it is. An easy slope is marked with a green circle. Green slopes are often wide and not very steep. A green slope is great for learning how to snowboard and for warming up at the start of an outing. An intermediate slope is marked with a blue square. Of course, your idea of intermediate may not match another person's. Some blue slopes have moguls. Other blue slopes are steep with sharp twists. Be prepared to test yourself when you decide to ride a blue slope. A black diamond slope is difficult. Black diamonds are designed for experts and advanced skiers and snowboarders. Black diamonds are steep and often narrow. Most black diamonds have moguls or crests. Black diamond slopes are often bordered by trees and steep ditches. Challenge yourself, but be smart. Stay on runs you can handle. Watch out for other snowboarders and skiers.

Snurfer held a rope attached to its front section.

Jake Burton began experimenting with snowboards in the early 1970s. Jake was a skier and surfer. He had been riding Snurfers since he was in high school. Jake worked at night at his job. He worked on snowboards during the day. He would carry his latest snowboard up the slopes of Stratton Mountain, Vermont. Once on top, he would strap the board to his boots and ride down. With each run, he learned more about snowboard design.

Jake decided that wood, not plastic, worked the best for the top of the snowboard. Plastic got too hard on cold days. The snowboard had to be flexible for a rider to control it. Jake also learned that snowboards need smooth, sharp, metal edges so the rider can make quick stops on icy snow. Jake put a tough, flexible plastic called P-tex, which skiers use, on the bottom of his snowboards. The P-tex reduced the friction between the board and the snow.

Jake also found that quick movements were easier on short boards. He decided to make a board that was longer than a skateboard and shorter than a surfboard. Jake spent hours in his workshop and hiking up mountains. But when he finished his snowboard, it was fast, safe, fun, and inexpensive to make. Best of all, his snowboard could do everything skis could do—and more!

But the reaction of others frustrated Jake. American ski resort owners still wouldn't let snowboarders ride their chairlifts. Chairlifts are machines that take people up and down a mountain. The resort owners thought snowboards were dangerous. Most ski shop owners refused to sell snowboards.

In places where surfing was

Jake Burton began snowboarding while in high school. Later, he researched and designed snowboards and created a company to manufacture them.

popular, however, snowboarding took off. Other snowboarders started their own companies. Soon the snowboard makers added new features and improved old ones. Riders now have dozens of models from which to choose.

Snowboards, like skis, need **bindings** to keep a rider's feet attached to the snowboard or ski. A good binding is sturdy enough to give the rider control but not so rigid that the rider would break a leg if he or she fell. Snowboard makers had trouble creating a good binding. By 1983, however, Jeff Grell had come up with a binding system that surrounded the snowboarder's foot with a hard plastic shell. The shell was clamped tightly to the board with straps and metal buckles. With these bindings, riders could control their snowboards even on **hard-pack.** Hardpack is the hard, icy snow found at most ski resorts.

By the mid-1990s, snow-boarders could ride at most of the ski areas in North America. Now there are snowboarders in at least 75 nations and on 5 continents. Snowboarding may be an event in the 2002 Winter Olympic Games.

Snowboards have changed a lot since the days of snurfing. Still, the basic pleasure of sliding down a mountain slope on a single, smooth board remains the same.

Tom Sims built a snowboard in his high school shop class. He has continued to develop snowboards for the last 30 years.

Chapter 2

BASICS

Equipment

The first step in learning how to ride a snowboard is choosing a snowboard. At any snowboard shop, you'll find an amazing variety of colors, shapes, and sizes.

A new snowboard costs several hundred dollars. Used snowboards are much cheaper. They're usually available at preseason ski-swaps and ski shops.

Most riders borrow a snowboard from another rider or rent one for their first time. Whether you're borrowing, renting, or buying, let a professional snowboarding instructor or an experienced rider help you choose which model is right for you.

13

The Snowboard

This diagram of a snowboard shows its parts and explains their uses:

Nose: The front, or leading, end of the snowboard. Rounded, upturned shape reduces friction by pushing snow under, rather than over, the board. Also called the shovel.

Heelside edge: The edge on the same side as the snowboarder's heels. For carving backside turns, down-mountain stopping and traversing.

Bindings: Fasteners that hold the snowboarder's feet onto the snowboard. **Mounting Sockets** (not shown): The drill holes that hold the bindings to the snowboard with screws.

Leash: Fastens around rider's leg to prevent runaway snowboards.

Stomp Pad: Provides friction for rear foot when riding out of back binding.

Toeside edge: The edge on the same side as the snowboarder's toes. For carving frontside turns, up-mountain stopping and traversing.

Tail: The rear, or trailing, end of the snowboard. A board with a shovel tail may be ridden either direction.

Freestyle snowboard

Use a snowboard that's right for what you want to do with it. If you're a skateboarder, for instance, you may want to do turns and jumps. A **freestyle** snowboard is short and flexible. It has a **shovel** on both ends and low-backed bindings. With a freestyle snowboard, you can do your skateboarding tricks on the snow. If you want to ride in snow up to your neck, choose an **alpine** board. This board will be long, narrow, and stiff. An alpine board has high-backed bindings and a squared or **asymmetrical** tail. You will stand sideways on the snowboard, so pick a board that is about as wide as your feet are long. That way, your toes and heels won't dig into the snow during turns. Boards vary in

Alpine snowboard

Snowboard Art

In any snowboard shop, you will see many different ways of decorating snowboards. Some snowboard designs are so eye-catching that you may want a board for what it looks like, rather than for what it can do. The sketch or painting on the snowboard shouldn't be your first reason for buying it, but the art can be the top tiebreaker!

Snowboard makers hire artists to create drawings and paintings for the snowboards. Sometimes these works are one-of-a-kind originals. Other times they are mass-produced.

In 1990 Morrow Snowboards hired Scott Clum to create graphics displays. Clum has inspired many artists to use the snowboard for self-expression.

Professional snowboard artists often spend much of their time riding their snowboards. They get their inspiration from the mountain.

length from about 4 feet to almost 6 feet. Children and short adults use smaller snowboards than taller riders. Also, the heavier the rider, the stiffer the board needs to be.

Next, decide which foot will be your lead foot. When you're batting in a baseball or softball game, which foot is closest to the pitcher? That's probably the foot you want in the forward binding. Snowboarders call a stance in which the rider's right foot is forward a **goofy** stance. A stance in which the snowboarder's left foot is forward is called a **regular** stance.

Goofy stance

Regular stance

Clothing

When getting dressed for snowboarding, wear layers of clothing. That way, when you get hot, you can take off a layer. If you get cold, you can add a layer. It's better to be a little overdressed because you can't add a layer that you don't have. Here are some ideas for your layers:

Layer one: Thermal tops and bottoms made of a wool-and-cotton blend or a synthetic fabric, such as polypropylene. These blends keep you warm even when they're wet.

Layer two: Lightweight wool sweater and pants. Don't wear cotton. Cotton is comfortable, but it won't keep you warm when it gets wet.

Layer three: Water-resistant snowpants and jacket, lined for warmth. Riders often wear long jackets to keep snow out of their pants.

Your most important clothing choices are socks, gloves, and boots. Your fingers and toes are the first body parts to be frostbitten. Most riders wear two pairs of wool socks.

Mittens are a good choice. Gloved fingers freeze faster than fingers in mittens. Since 90 percent of your body heat is lost through your head, the old woodsman's saying holds true for snowboarding: *If your fingers or toes get cold, put on a hat.* Always wear a hat.

Snowboarders can fly down the slopes without changing into hard-shell boots, as skiers must. Many riders choose boots that are made for snowboarding. Boots should be snug around heels and ankles to prevent blisters. A loose-fitting boot increases the chance of injuring your ankles and knees. Don't tie your boots too tightly, however. Boots tied too tightly will cause numb feet and frozen toes.

Fast snowboarding can make your vision blurry. Ice pellets or snow can sting your eyes and force them shut. You can prevent these problems by wearing goggles.

Where to Begin

Snowboarders are welcome at

A snowboarding boot looks like a regular winter boot.

most ski areas now, but you don't have to go to a resort for your first try at snowboarding. You can snowboard on small hills on public lands for free. On these hills, you won't have to worry about running into other riders and skiers. Hiking up the hills is an excellent way to loosen up and warm up your muscles.

Ski resorts do offer many advantages, however. Ski areas generally have some simple runs. Most ski areas have snowboards and boots available for you to rent. They often have instructors who give lessons. Most resorts make artificial snow, so you don't have to wait for nature to provide snow. With a chairlift to take you to the top, you can do many runs in a day. The more runs you make, the faster you will improve.

Take advantage of fresh snow

for your first few outings. Hardpack and ice are difficult surfaces on which to learn. If you can see brush, grass, or rocks, put off snowboarding until after the next big snow-storm. Six to 12 inches of new snow creates a soft cushion for you when you fall.

Strapping In

To get started, sit in the snow on a flat area. Put your front foot binding on first. Remove any snow or ice that is in the bindings. Tighten the fasteners as firmly as you can without feeling pain. Then fasten your back foot binding.

Unlike skateboarding, where you are free to move your feet, snowboarders must choose one stance that works for everything they want to do. Most bindings swivel in position after a few screws are loosened. After three or four runs, you will find the position that's right for you.

Now it's time to test your balance. Stand with your knees bent, your weight evenly balanced on both legs, and your shoulders facing forward. Lean over the nose of the board. Lean over the back. Rock onto your toe edge, and onto your heel edge. If you fall, you're doing it right. The limits of your balance are very small when you aren't moving. As you go faster, you will be able to lean farther away from the snowboard. At high speeds, you may even be able to touch your cheek to the snow!

Chapter 3

MANEUVERS

Snowboarders love to do wild and difficult tricks. But even the wildest trick starts with one of the following five simple moves.

Once you learn these five basic moves, you will be able to ride on many runs and make smooth turns. These five moves can be learned in a short time.

First, however, you must learn how to fall without hurting yourself. You will fall many times while you are learning to snowboard. Falling is a part of learning. Falling doesn't have to be painful, however. Doing a controlled fall helps to prevent an injury. If you're snowboarding on ice or hardpack, wear pads and a helmet for extra protection.

Controlled Fall

Leslee is doing a controlled fall. When Leslee feels she's going too fast, she leans as close to the ground as possible. She faces uphill and reaches for the snow with her hands.

She lets herself fall gradually onto the uphill side. At the same time, Leslee pushes her toeside edge of the snowboard into the snow to slow herself down.

Quick Fixes to Common Problems

I can't ride forward without the rear end of the snowboard sliding out.
The end of the snowboard that has more weight on it will be the end that goes downhill first. Try bending at your waist to shift your weight over the nose of the snowboard.

I can't stand on the board. I feel completely out of control.
Try crouching. Many new riders succeed in the crouch because their center of gravity is closer to the ground. Also, if you fall, you have less distance to travel before you hit the snow.

I can turn, but when I try to go back the other way, my board keeps going. I end up facing backward.
Lean your weight onto your front foot when turning. Now your back foot can push the snowboard the other way. Although both feet are tied to the same board, they act independently.
Beginners often don't want to lean forward because they're afraid of going too fast. But the front edge of the snowboard has to slide downslope in order to slow down again on the other edge. In other words, when making turns for speed control, you have to speed up before you can slow down. Always look in the direction you want to turn.

What do I do with my hands when snowboarding?
There is no right or wrong way to hold your arms. To start, try holding your fists near your chest, like a boxer. Keep your arms loose and relaxed.

Stop

The first step in learning to ride a snowboard is learning how to stop without falling. Amy is doing a **backside** stop.

Amy twists at her waist and looks in the direction she wants her snowboard to point. She puts most of her weight on her front foot so she can kick the board around. She leans uphill, opposite the direction she's going. As she slows down, Amy slowly shifts her weight so it's balanced on both legs.

Sideslip

Riding sideways down the slope is called doing a **sideslip**. A snowboarder can sideslip on the toeside or the heelside. Sabrina is doing a toeside sideslip.

Sabrina stands sideways to the run with her weight on her toe edge. She straightens her legs slightly and turns her ankles toward her heel edge. As her toe edge comes out of the snow, her board begins to glide. When she wants to stop, she puts more weight back on her toe edge.

Traverse

To go across a hill, a rider uses a **traverse**. Sabrina balances over the uphill edge. Then she puts a little more of her weight on her front foot than on her back foot. Sabrina keeps her uphill edge down to keep herself moving.

Skid

If a rider wants to slow down while going straight down the slope, the rider can do a **skid**. Trevor shifts most of his weight to his front foot. With his back foot, he kicks out the tail of his board. Then Trevor crouches to

keep his balance and leans on his toe edge.

A skid can also be used to turn. By putting his weight on the uphill edge and alternating heel edge and toe edge, Trevor can make a series of turns.

Riding a Chairlift

Riding a chairlift is a quick and easy way to get to the top of the mountain. Getting on and off the lift can be tricky at first.

Take your rear foot out of the binding before getting on the lift. Keep that foot loose until you are clear of the lift at the top. You won't be allowed on the chairlift unless you have a **leash** attached to your front binding and fastened around your leg.

When the riders in front of you have left the ground, move forward to the load line. Look over your shoulder for the chair. The lift operator will catch the chair to make it easier for you to load. Grab the chair. Sit back and lower the safety bar, if there is one.

As you approach the peak, signs will warn you when you should get ready to get off the lift. There will be a mound of snow at the top.

With your front foot, point the nose of the snowboard toward the sky. Slide your rear foot solidly against the rear binding on the **stomp pad**. Let your board glide naturally onto the mound. When the bottom of your snowboard rests entirely on the snow, stand up. Push away from the chair and ride the slope. If you fall, scramble away from the unloading area.

Carve

A **carve** leaves a thin track in the snow rather than the wide trail left by a skid. A rider must ride fast, however, to carve.

Jimmy, at left, is doing a heel-side carve. He has most of his weight on the front of the board. He presses his heel edge into the snow. Jimmy balances all his weight against the momentum of the board, cutting a sharp groove.

Dylan, below, is doing a toe-side carve. He presses his toe edge into the snow.

Going Flat Out

Sometimes a snowboarder needs to travel across a flat area. If the rider has to move slowly, in the lift line, for example, the rider won't have enough momentum to glide. Then the snowboarder does a move called **skating**. This skating isn't like ice skating. It's like skateboarding.

To skate, take your rear foot out of the binding. Lean on your front foot and bend your front knee. Lift your rear foot as if you were taking a normal step and pull the board forward. Small steps usually work best. When you have taken three or four steps, you may have gained enough momentum to ride a short distance. Place your rear foot on the stomp pad and glide.

Chapter 4

COMPETITIVE SNOWBOARDING

When snowboarders want to compete, they may enter either freestyle or race contests, or both. There are two freestyle events, and five race events.

In the freestyle events, the snowboarders do tricks. Judges award the riders points for their routines. In the races, the snowboarders are timed.

Snowboard racers wear tight bodysuits to go as fast as they can. Racers also wear hard-shell boots to protect their ankles while making sharp turns. Snowboarders in **giant slalom** and **super G** races must wear helmets.

Riders in **slalom** events wear shoulder pads, face masks, and shin pads to protect themselves when they smash into the gates. All competitors wear bibs with numbers.

The United States Amateur Snowboard Association runs amateur competitions in the United States. The USASA groups snowboarders according to age. Boys and girls 12 years old and younger compete in one category. In the other groups, boys and girls compete in separate events:

Division	Ages
J3	13-14
J2	15-16
J1	17-18
Seniors	19-25
Masters	26-35
Legends	36-49
Methuselahs	50 and older

Freestyle Competition

● *Halfpipe*

A **halfpipe** is a big ditch dug into the snow. Its walls rise 7 to 14 feet on either side. A halfpipe is about 250 to 350 feet long.

Snowboarders glide down one side of the halfpipe and up the other. Sometimes the riders flip into the air. Snowboarders call that **catching air**.

● *Slopestyle*

A **slopestyle** course is filled with challenges. Each snowboarder chooses his or her course. While riding the course, each snowboarder does tricks.

A **railslide** is one type of obstacle on a slopestyle course. A railslide is a metal or wooden bar, or a downed tree. A snowboarder rides on the railslide. A quarterpipe, which is a halfpipe with just one wall, is another obstacle riders may face.

● *Judging*

Freestyle judges sit on a platform at the bottom of the run. Three, four, or five judges score the events. Riders perform twice. The judges add together a rider's two scores. The rider with the highest score wins.

The judges give riders points for how well they do their tricks. The judges also look for a smooth ride with unusual moves. If a snowboarder falls, he or she loses points.

Race Competition

● *Slalom*

Competitors in a slalom race must ride through a series of gates as they go swiftly down a slope. The gates are marked with red and blue poles. There are 30 to 70 gates. Racers are timed as they take two trips, or runs, down the slope. The runs are on different courses. The snowboarder's two times are added. The racer with the fastest total time wins.

● *Parallel Slalom*

Two courses are set up, side by side, for the **parallel slalom.** Snowboarders are grouped into pairs to race, two at a time. Racers with odd numbers race on the right course for the first run. Racers with even numbers race on the left course for the first run. They switch courses for the second run. The racer with the best total time wins.

● Giant Slalom

A giant slalom race is held on a steeper slope than a slalom race. The course is also longer. A giant slalom gate consists of two poles, one on either side. The poles are held together by banners. The gates are connected by red, then blue, banners.

Racers ride two runs. For the second run, some gates are placed in different positions. The racer with the fastest total time is the winner.

● Super G

A super G course is on a very steep slope. Racers must make wide and medium turns. The gates are set up across the full width of the run. Super G racers take only one run.

● Race Rules

A racer has to have both feet on the snowboard when passing a gate. The entire snowboard must cross the gate line. If a rider misses a gate, he or she must either go back through the gate or leave the course.

A racer may be disqualified for the following:
- missing a gate
- having an early or late start
- not passing the finish line with at least one foot on the snowboard
- accepting help from somebody else during a run
- not leaving the course promptly after completing a run.

Chapter 5

PRACTICE, PRACTICE

Beginning snowboarders fall as often as babies learning to walk. Having both feet tied onto a snowboard feels very strange. If you lose your balance, you can't just take a foot off to steady yourself as skateboarders do. Most people, however, begin to feel at ease after one or two days of snowboarding.

Snowboarding is fun, and it's great exercise. Snowboarding conditions your entire body, from heart and lungs to the muscles of your stomach, legs, and even arms.

Conditioning

Janine has come to Mount Hood for summer snowboard camp. Before going up the mountain, she stretches the muscles of her legs, arms, back, and neck. Stretching helps prevent injuries.

Janine keeps in shape at home by doing strengthening exercises. One exercise that strengthens her legs is the wall-sit. Janine is demonstrating a wall-sit in the bottom photo on this page. To do a wall-sit, Janine leans her back and head against a wall. Then she sits as if there were a chair beneath her. She holds this position for one minute. She takes a one-minute rest and then does it again.

Next Janine hikes up a small hill. She runs down, taking long steps. She wants to keep her control, not run as fast as she can. Janine does this three or

four times. Wall-sits and down-hill runs work the leg muscles snowboarders use while riding. Sit-ups and chin-ups are other good exercises.

Janine also does activities that help her lungs and heart work better. Bicycling, swim-ming, and jogging are some of her favorites.

Balance, control, and flexibil-ity are some of the skills used in waterskiing, surfing, skate-boarding, and gymnastics. These skills are also used while snowboarding.

Ways to Practice

Once you can do the basic moves, you can work on several skills at once. These three drills will help you improve your ability to turn, slow down, speed up, and stop.

● *Downhill to Sideslip*

Trevor wants to ride forward while keeping his speed under

control. To practice this, he rides downhill, then sideways, and then downhill again.

Trevor chooses an easy slope. He starts in the sideslip position. When he is ready to ride downhill, he shifts his weight onto his front foot. He kicks the snowboard uphill with his back foot. When Trevor wants to slow down, he shifts his weight back onto his front foot. Then he kicks his rear foot downhill and digs his heel edge into the snow.

● *Traverse to Skidding Turn*

Trevor puts most of his weight on his toe edge. At the side of the hill, he twists at his waist and looks at the other side. Trevor shifts his weight onto his front foot. He kicks his rear foot out until his heel edge catches the snow on the uphill side. Next, he balances his weight evenly on both legs on his heel edge.

● *Downhill to Skid to Stop*

Amy has trouble stopping without falling so she is practicing these easy steps. She begins by riding downhill. As she goes faster, she shifts some of her weight over the snowboard's nose. Slowly, she slides her back foot downhill while putting more pressure on her heel.

As Amy turns sideways to the slope, she balances her weight on both legs. She leans uphill in a skid. As she slows, she leans over the top of the snowboard until she stops.

Chapter 6

STUNTS

Snowboarders love to dream up new tricks and improve old ones. Talented riders leap and twist gracefully, almost like dancers. On a snowboard, there is always something new to learn.

Excellent snowboarders ride equally well, no matter which foot is in the lead. They switch effortlessly—left foot first, then right one.

One skill a freestyle snowboarder needs to have is the ability to ride backward. This is known as riding **fakie**, or in a **switch-stance**.

Super Snowboarder

Before Craig Kelly retired from professional snowboard competition in 1991, he had won four world championships and three overall U.S. titles. Craig still snowboards. He also rides a mountain bike.

Craig grew up in Mount Vernon, Washington, near Mount Baker. As a child, Craig dreamed of playing professional baseball. He didn't go skiing until he was 15. Later that year, he went snowboarding. Craig instantly loved snowboarding. He and his friends rode at every chance. They helped each other create new moves.

Craig competed in his first contest in 1984. He finished fourth. Just two years later, Craig won the World Slalom Championship.

Fakie

The quickest way to learn to ride fakie is to ride with your rear foot in front for entire days. This method takes about as much time and effort as learning to ride in the first place. You will fall often again, so do this only on soft snow.

Another way to learn to ride fakie is to practice the **alternating traverse**. In this drill, Trevor slides side to side down the hill.

He doesn't make turns. Instead, he switches his lead foot by shifting his weight from right to left. He puts most of his weight on whichever foot is first. When Trevor is ready to change direction, he bends his front knee and straightens his back leg.

Meet Michele Taggert

Home: Salem, Oregon

How she started snowboarding: Michelle watched her big brother ride for a couple of years before she tried it herself. She entered a halfpipe contest her third time on a snowboard. "I loved catching airs," Michelle said. "I just threw myself up the walls and launched as high as I could. Then I'd crash back down in the pipe and do it again. The judges liked my aggressiveness and I won!"

Turning pro: When she was 18, Michelle became a professional.

Top career honor: She won the 1993-94 World All-Around Championship. "It was my goal to become world champion," Michelle said, "but I hadn't planned on it happening so soon."

Advice to beginning riders: "Don't give up after one or two times. At first it's frustrating, but after that, just have a good time."

Railslide

A railslide is a bar, like a handrail along a staircase, or a dead tree. A snowboarder rides over the railslide and launches off it.

Dylan uses a skid to approach the railslide. Once on the railslide, Dylan rides as he would normally. When he gets to the end of the railslide, he twists at the waist and pushes off with his legs.

In the air, Dylan's snowboard follows in the direction of his twist. To stop the turn, he looks at where he wants to land. He lowers the rear of his snowboard first to avoid a face-first fall. Falling off a railslide can hurt. Practice this move only after a heavy snow. Check first for hidden obstructions.

Launch

Anything that causes a snow-boarder to become airborne is a **launch.** Cliffs, boulders, and downed trees all can be used as launches. Going off a launch and catching air can be a big thrill. It can also be a big problem. Before you take a launch, ride over the landing area two or three times. Check for rocks, trees, or other obstructions.

After you've checked the area, you're ready to fly. Keep in mind that a safe landing starts with a good approach. As you near the top of the launch, slow down. Bend your knees and hips to get as close to the ground as possible.

When landing, put the rear end of your snowboard down first. Landing tail first prevents the nose of the board from digging into the snow and throwing the rider into a wild cartwheel.

Powder and Back Country

For snowboarders, there is no such thing as too much snow. Riding on deep **powder** can feel like floating if the snow is fresh and light. To ride deep powder, you have to have a steep slope. If you don't go fast, you can't stay on top of the snow.

Steep, powdery slopes are often found in the back country,

Snowboard Parks

Many ski resorts have a special section for snowboarders to meet, practice tricks, and learn from each other. Snowboard parks feature halfpipes, quarterpipes, jumps, platforms, railslides, and slalom courses. Many parks have "snowboarders only" towropes. By getting up the hill quickly, snowboarders can practice a trick many times, or invent new moves.

Snowboard parks can be found at many ski areas. Snowboarders in the Midwest can practice the same tricks as riders in Colorado or Utah.

not the trampled runs of ski resorts. Whenever you ride in the back country, ride with a partner. Tell someone else where you're going. Also, check with park rangers or the ski patrol skiers about avalanches or other dangers.

To stay on top of powder, you must lean heavily on your rear foot. This keeps the nose of your board from sinking into the snow. Your rear leg will get tired quickly, so turn often. When you turn, you will have to shift your weight forward. This will give your rear leg a rest. Then you will be able to ride without stopping. Try to avoid stopping in such deep snow because getting started again may be difficult.

Snowboarding in the woods can be exciting. Before entering the woods, find out from a local rider where you will finish. It's no fun to find a deep river full of cold water. Always ride with a partner and tell someone else where you're going.

Snowboarding is a fun sport. It's also a sport that is changing quickly. You can have a part in shaping this amazing pastime.

SNOWBOARDING TALK

alpine: A style of snowboard designed for flowing curves and high speeds.

alternating traverse: A drill in which the snowboarder draws a falling-leaf pattern with the snowboard as he or she goes down the slope. Used when learning to ride fakie.

asymmetrical: Not the same on both sides. An asymmetrical snowboard is designed for speed and ease in alpine-style carving turns.

backside: Maneuvers that are done on the heelside edge when the rider is facing downhill.

binding: A device that holds a rider's foot to a snowboard.

carve: To turn sharply on the snowboard's edge without sliding. A carved turn leaves a thin track in the snow.

catching air: To become airborne or take flight on a snowboard.

fakie: To ride down the hill with the snowboarder's rear foot going first. Also called **switch-stance.**

freestyle: A competitive event in which riders do a variety of moves using railslides, bumps, halfpipes, and other tricks.

giant slalom: A competitive event in which riders race down a course with gates. The racers choose their own paths through the widely dispersed gates.

goofy: A riding stance in which the snowboarder's right foot is forward.

halfpipe: A rounded channel dug out of the snow. Riders use the side walls as launches for catching air and performing tricks.

hardpack: Snow that has been compressed into ice or become choppy and hard.

launch: A cliff or other formation used by snowboarders to become airborne.

leash: A rope or band attached to the front binding and fastened around a snowboarder's leg to prevent runaway snowboards.

parallel slalom: A competitive race in which two snowboarders ride identical side-by-side courses at the same time.

powder: Soft, fresh snow.

railslide: A wooden or metal rail or a downed tree that snowboarders slide on and use to become airborne.

regular: A riding stance in which the snowboarder's left foot is in the lead.

shovel: The rounded, upturned tip of the snowboard.

sideslip: To go down a run with the snowboard sideways on the slope.

skating: A pushing motion, similar to skateboarding, that snowboarders use on flat surfaces.

skid: A maneuver in which the snowboarder puts more weight on the uphill edge to control his or her speed without stopping or turning.

slalom: A competitive race in which riders race against time through a course of gates.

slopestyle: A competitive freestyle event in which snowboarders do tricks off launches and obstacles.

stomp pad: The pad installed on a snowboard to provide friction when the snowboarder's foot is riding out of the rear binding.

super G: A competitive race event in which snowboarders do a variety of medium and long turns across the entire slope. An abbreviation of super giant slalom.

switch-stance: A riding technique in which the snowboarder goes down the hill with his or her rear foot in the lead. Also called riding **fakie.**

traverse: To move back and forth across the slope.

FOR MORE INFORMATION

Alpine Surf Wear
605 Bank Street
Wallace, ID 83873

Bored Magazine
364 North 77th Street
Seattle, WA 98103

Burton Snowboards
P. O. Box 4449
Burlington, VT 05406-4449

Gnu, Lib-tech Snowboards
2600 West Commodore Way
Seattle, WA 98199

International Snowboard Federation
P. O. Box 477
Vail, CO 81658

National Snowboard Inc.
P. O. Box 1168
Conifer, CO 80433

Snowboard Educators of North
America
4352 Onyx Point
Eagan, MN 55122

Snowboard Magazine
2814 Fairfield Avenue, Suite 137
Bridgeport, CT 06605

Snowboarder Magazine
P. O. Box 1028
Dana Point, CA 92629

TransWorld SNOWboarding Magazine
353 Airport Road
Oceanside, CA 92054

United States Amateur Snowboard
Association (USASA)
c/o Chuck Allen
P. O. Box 8251
Green Valley Lake, CA 92341

United States Snowboarding Team
1500 Kearns Boulevard
P. O. Box 100
Park City, UT 84060

FURTHER READING

Althen, K.C. *The Complete Book of Snowboarding*. Rutland, Vt.: Charles E. Tuttle Company, Inc., 1990.

Garcia, Elena. *A Beginner's Guide to Zen and the Art of Snowboarding*. Berkeley, Calif.: Amberco Press, 1990.

McMullen, John. *The Basic Essentials of Snowboarding*. Merrillville, Ind.: ICS Books, Inc., 1991.

Reichenfeld, Rob, and Anna Bruechert. *Snowboarding*. Champaign, Ill.: Human Kinetics Publishers, Inc., 1995.

INDEX

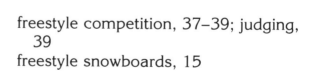